Still Time

Reflections on Aging

Still Time

Reflections on Aging

Kathleen Serley

Cover design by Shay Culligan
Cover image by Dawid Zawila on Unsplash

ISBN: 978-1-63980-830-4

Kelsay Books
502 South 1040 East, A-119
American Fork, Utah 84003
Kelsaybooks.com

Acknowledgments

Thank you to the following publications, where these poems have appeared, some in slightly different versions.

ArtasPoetryasArt exhibit 2022: "November"

Bramble, Summer 2023: "Dilly Beans"

Eastern Iowa Review, 2022: "Hey, Neighbor"

Trout Museum of Art, exhibit 2025: "Reedmace"

Verse Wisconsin, online 2010: "All Badge Wearers"

WFOP Museletter, 2019: "A Walk in the Woods"

Wisconsin Poets' Calendar, 2016: "Retired"

Wisconsin Poets' Calendar, 2024: "Sand Castles"

Contents

Dilly Beans

He died in late June   my friend's friend   just as the garden
beans were pushing their way above ground stretching
toward the sun   my friend found his recipe for dilly beans
in a cupboard handed it to me   I folded it squaring up the
corners wedged it into the crease of a card with golden
squash blossoms pictured on the front   gave it along with
the empty quart jars lining my pantry shelves to a young
neighbor   she likes to garden to cook   her kids love dilly
beans

Hey, Neighbor

Remember the year we moved to the country
you to a spent farm   I to a cut-over 80
two city-bred back-to-the-landers bent on stewardship
the trees calling us   calling our families

>*Seeker, let the trees guide you*
>*listen to the rustling of their leaves*

We breathed easier among the trees
quieted beneath their canopy
breathing in as they breathed out
we settled, accepting the woods as equal player

>*hear hope in the woodpecker's rat-tatting*
>*heed caution in a crow's warning caw*

It would take us fifty years
to speak of carbon sequestering
fifty years to talk
about the caterpillars hosted by our oaks

>*follow the crisscrossing deer trails*
>*alert to discovery on winding paths*

But in all that time we welcomed the coolness
of the woods in mid-summer, admired the burnished
beauty of those oaks in fall   we thinned and planted
planted and thinned shaping the woods

> *enjoy wild apple trees in full bloom*
> *alert to porcupines swaying from the treetops*

Today, I see you from my fence line setting off down
that old logging road on an autumn walk among your trees
stewards in their own right, they stand tall across the land
sentinels to your trek as evening shadows lengthen

> *match your breath to the forest*
> *adjust your pace to lengthening shadows*

A Lament on Aging

One day my body will give out putting unease to rest.
All thought of what might bring me to my knees will stand at rest.

Is ache a sign of pending doom? Will one pain seal my fate?
Such worrying makes old age a tease I must put to rest.

I shall not be tempted to shed my hair to gain a day,
or so I say. A mantra that repeats without a rest.

It's the slow decline I fear, not falling flat.
Diminished by a long disease before my final rest.

I fear giving up my place; cared for rather than to care.
Hearing, memory, sight lost by degrees make me long for rest.

How can I give up driving, leave my gardens, forfeit my home.
Who will I be without these things? That question will not rest.

I want to be the one to host, to share advice, to help.
Yet, I am sidelined; the culture decrees it's time to rest.

Make a place for me as seer, an elder to respect.
Sage Kate, my years an asset. Laud them, please, as I near rest.

All Badge Wearers

Yesterday, a man walked toward me
he hurried along the busy street
wind tossing his name badge high across his chest
passing me he smiled distantly
absorbed in his brief escape from the office

In recognition I reached for my own lanyard
to straighten my ID to introduce myself
as fellow employee keeping step with work's agenda

But my identification was missing
retired to a bureau drawer
and with it those quick strides taking me forward
to team meetings and project proposals
accomplishments recognized by all badge wearers

Who am I now adrift at noon
without my name badge for anchor.

Retired

I seek perspective
clear contrasts in
black and white but
light chases dark
focal points fade
shadows limit my view

Accustomed to images
confined to flat screens
I struggle to tease shape
from unfocused light

November

Late November I sit in the garden a slanted
sun warming my face spiked shadows of barren

blueberry bushes play along the wall
crumpled ferns fold over the path dark-eyed

juncos scavenge for seed   I will plant
the French climbing beans again next year

they flourished along the fence

Reedmace in the Marsh

I drove the river road this morning
followed the dark, churning water
against its current to the river's beginnings,
a marshy wetland sprouting Reedmace

I love this marsh, especially in spring
when red-winged blackbirds claim it
calling from atop the frayed seed heads
filling the space with sound and color

But I have come today for the quiet
after a year of surgeries, days filled
with appointments rather than adventures
I crave connection with this life source

This place where rain water is held and released
held and released as nature's pulse beat
the water cleansed through the reeds' long roots
and sent downstream to speed the river's mission

This place where beavers forage on the reeds and
muskrats salvage the stalks to build their homes
where birds feast and insects flourish and the Reedmace
stands tall, a firmly rooted sentinel of the marsh

I have come today to slow my breathing in this
brown and white world to steady my feet on level ground
to stand a little straighter in the way of the Reedmace
dream a new day as a winter sun blues the sky

Haiku

Fall's busy squirrels
pad their cache from future want
I work to spend mine

Still Time

Here and there a dry leaf
scuttles across the road
drawing my attention downward
from the brooding sky to where
sequestering roots keep soil from
shifting in the scuttling wind

I step around and over these
crab-walking leaves reluctant
to crush even one underfoot
the exercise bringing to mind
my own diminishing mobility
the seasons running out

But all of a sudden the wind
picks up speed tossing leaves
high above my head
playful as a child and I dare
to believe there is still time
to let my heart soar

Sand Castles

Thanks for texting the pics of your day at the beach with
the boys how fun to see their happy faces   you looked
much the same at that age, swinging your pail helping
to carry the tote   I alongside mirroring your widening
smile   we'd set up "camp" in that sweet spot between
sun-baked earth and water ankle-deep where pulsing
tides polished the sand leaving it moist as wet cement
perfect for shaping our castles   shoulder to shoulder
we filled pail after pail mounding them to towers and
turrets   digging deep to dredge the moat, sand clinging
to our fingers and toes   the lapping water trapped before
it eroded our foundation

In shift to sideline
I scroll through your pics ever
heart set alongside

Halloween

All Saints' Eve and the spooks are coming,
skipping up my drive loot bags held aloft
to the porch where I sit treat bowl beside me.
Who have we here, I say by way of hello.

Skipping up my drive loot bags held aloft
they call out names I've not heard.
Who have we here, I repeat as my greeting.
Names from movies I've not seen tumble out.

They call out names I've not heard.
Where is Cinderella, Snow White, Snoopy, but no
names from movies I've not seen tumble out.
I feel old, out of place, left out of the mix.

Where is Cinderella, Snow White, Snoopy, but no
I meet girls brandishing swords and straight purple hair.
I feel old, out of place, left out of the mix.
No friendly ghosts here, just zombies and more.

I meet girls brandishing swords and straight purple hair.
How can this be, I've grown too old for this day.
No friendly ghosts here, just zombies and more
reminding me of a future I choose to ignore.

How can this be, I've grown too old for this day.
What happened to Elmo, Ernie and Big Bird, the best.
Reminded of a future I choose to ignore,
I'm out of the loop I tell a dad held in tow.

What happened to Elmo, Ernie and Big Bird, the best.
Who have we here. The answers blur past me.
I'm out of the loop I tell a dad held in tow.
Meet Batman, he says, lifting his toddler. *Ah, Batman,* I say.

All These Years

I sit at the back of the church an empty
pew in front of me, the wall behind for brace.
After three years away, of Zoom and masking,
they sing again and I return to listen.
This historic choir mingling as one voice,
song of the town   fifty years   part of my life.

Fifty years slipped away, yet it seems my life's
but started; that just yesterday new, empty,
unexplored spaces opened to my young voice.
I settle into the pew, their songs embrace
me gifting friendship, calling me to listen
for counsel, for connection. Unmasking

vibes loosed by the beat of memory unmasked,
a string of veiled images, a long-awaited life
one job, then another, two, three. Stop. Listen.
Frame after frame   birth, death, an empty
nest filled again by two grand gifts   all things braced
by the steadying sound of a loved one's voice.

I think I hear my friend's voice.
She flanked by friends   faces masked
in kinship's glow   their own voices
extended outward as life
joins us in this near empty
pew   their friend's my friend. Listen.

Fifty years and more. I have learned to listen
to the red bird's song, the wind's vibrato. Voice
overs to the workday's din, ever-empty
sounds cast as false comfort attempts to mask
a wandering purpose the void left by life's
relentless push ahead. Despite all, I brace

myself for the luge ride. Eyes wide open, feet braced
against the back of the church pew, I listen
to this choir calling me from thought to life
in the moment centered here by their voices
friends I have known for these fifty years masked,
unmasked connections defying emptiness.

In my seventh decade, I welcome life's embrace
seek empty times, opportunities to listen
hope to give voice to all I carry masked, unmasked.

Haiku

Monday's leftovers
served on my Sunday dishes
no reason to wait

How Are You, My Dear

It seems to many I have grown dear.
Receptionists and salesclerks all grin
and greet this sweet endearment falsely shared.
Am I to them a person dear or just
someone identified by graying hair
an elder needing special verbal care.
It sounds to me like talking down to age.
Assuming what? That age alone disowns?

A better plan to meet my eyes omit
the dear when saying hi. Connect with me
by real talk: "Can you believe this day,"
and I will say, "It looks to me like years
when apples bent the orchard trees to ground."
What comes to mind on such a day for you?

My Time

We'll go to the light when our time comes, my friend says
She's looking forward to it

Not me

I don't want to float around in a swath of light
unreachable above the clouds

I have things to do

down here

I intend to stay   to start over
do some things I missed this time around

Like those seven kids I postponed
while high on the feminist movement's wild ride

or that heirloom orchard planted in time
for me to enjoy the harvest

I like Earth with all its messiness
There's always something to do

Advocate for student lunches   Worry about water quality
March for world peace, human rights, border reform
Rise up at the mention of a book ban

Who needs all that light
I'm good with shade

I like watching the play of shadows over an open field,
the patterns of sun filtered through a tree canopy

Yes, indeed—I intend to be back,
grateful for another chance.

A Time for Repairs

High winds
snap a weak limb
from the old pine next door
just as I lose parts, hips and knees
aging

Haiku

Not spring's loud hurrah
winter snows come quietly
we are caught off guard

Dear Friend

With a nod to Ellen Kort, Wisconsin's first poet laureate

Reading Ellen Kort's *Letter from McCarty's Farm,*
I think to call you to say read this and we will talk
we first met in an Ellen class, remember
you a seasoned poet well-known on her circuit
I a newcomer relieved to snag a coveted slot

But you have passed beyond the reach of my intended call
beyond the time when we would while away an afternoon
talking the craft, the business, the art of poetry
leaving me untethered to shape these words alone

Where have you gone
that the constant question of our endless talks
when we didn't think it mattered when we always
had another day when leaving was about someone else

Walking in our city park, I look for you in the tree canopy
rooted near a century ago your lifetime but middle age
for them these trees will outlive children born today
if only we were more like trees

Some say you come with the cardinal perched
on the garden trellis but I sense you in the greetings I share
with my neighbors look for you in our open mics a tradition
we started together with a plate of cookies and a love of words

Ellen found the best in our workshopped poems
saying just the right thing nudging us to find our voices
reminded, I search for you in the poems you left with me
listen for your voice in the cadence of those verses
take heart from the connection, poetry's ageless gift

December

December the lake freezes hemmed on all sides
        its thrumming stilled
Shape the shore, form an eddy or flow downstream
        that time has passed
Last spring, I kayaked the current
        now I wait, my life on hold

Big Storm Coming

Hunker down   stock up
the weatherman says
five inches of snow by mid-day
stay put

I've been thinking of moving to a condo
no lawn   no stairs   no garden
pulling up roots   settling closer to my children
or checking out a warmer clime

I've been thinking of renting a storage unit
of going houseless   but what to store
the Windsor chair or the ladder back rocker
bookcases or blanket chests

Can I get by without
that *25-years of service* coffee mug
the lobster trap I bought
forty years ago on a trip to Maine

I keep thinking of moving while I can still move
before weeds claim my garden and stairs claim my knees
I watch for a sign   wait for the storm
stocked up   hunkered down   staying put

Life Cycle

As a child, I meandered my neighborhood
losing myself in sidewalk adventures
my parents just a step behind
until I sprinted ahead, a young woman
craving an adrenaline rush
rounding the track, beating my time
when of a sudden I settled into strolling
my toddler and I waving to neighbors
counting boulevard trees along the way
even when he ran ahead
I strolled park paths and nature trails
wondering at the busy lives of squirrels
'til taken by surprise, I slowed
poles for support, eyeing the end of the block
hoping not to lose myself along the way

      meandering

hoping not to lose myself along the way
poles for support, eyeing the end of the block
'til taken by surprise, I slowed
wondering at the busy lives of squirrels
I strolled park paths and nature trails
even when my son ran ahead
counting the boulevard trees along the way
my toddler and I waved to neighbors
when of a sudden I'd settled into strolling

after rounding the track, beating my time
craving an adrenaline rush
a young woman sprinting ahead
my parents just a step behind
losing myself in sidewalk adventures
I meandered my neighborhood, as a child.

A Walk in the Woods

I remember walking in the woods
and coming upon the mother bear with her twins
a porcupine climbing high
the tree swaying under his prickly weight

I remember the opening in the forest
the immigrant's empty cabin
his yard a carpet of violets
a wild apple tree in full bloom

I remember the fall we made apple jelly
on a stolen day, the filled jars aglow
like a captured September sun

Remember when we hung trail signs named
for your ninjas, the Michelangelo loop
Donatello's straight stretch through the heart of the woods

I will remember this day, walking in the woods
with your sons, the forest cut-over the big trees gone
we looked for seedling oaks four leaves, eight leaves, ten
when they finally form a canopy, remember.

Haiku

Cut loose to coast—yet
I've been busy this morning
listening to the rain

The Gift

I opened your gift today
lifted it from the box slipped it on
        For forty years I lived a list
        meetings carpools lunch-on-demand
at first I thought it didn't fit
it seemed too loose too open at the neck
        Uneasy in the stretch of time
        I feared a day without plan
I wear collars tend toward belts and ties
reluctant to embrace the shapeless shift
        Don't retire friends advised
        doubting my skills to fill the hours
but to my surprise I quite fancy the way it
drapes takes shape moves with me as I walk
        Surprising them, I quite enjoy
        a day to fashion as my own

Empty Nest

Silence sighs toward
turning leaves, turning on us
clamor for quiet
Seasons of focused chaos
idled into empty days.

Hummingbirds

My son is a warrior after drill remembers to stop for milk
swings by daycare to claim his child for dinner and a bath
on their way home calls me *what did you do today*   how
can I tell him about my afternoon the hummingbirds in my
garden

rows of flying geese
pieced in the corner of
batik by the yard

October

Late October's golden leaves hold fast to limbs in sprays.
Should I worry, not enjoy the presence of these leaves
kept from falling by the warmth of extra days.

Climate change eventually may set the world ablaze,
so perhaps the beauty of this grace time deceives
as late October's golden leaves hold fast to limbs in sprays.

But I choose to bask in the glory of the rays,
seize this special time to laugh not grieve,
keep from falling by the warmth of extra days.

Big storm coming my friends are wont to say.
"He died." "She's sick." I remind myself to breathe.
Watch late October's golden leaves hold fast to limbs in sprays.

Will the earth whither? Will I succumb? Worry weighs.
Yet, I embrace this lengthening season, want to believe
I'll keep from falling by the warmth of extra days.

When in time a chill wind shakes these branches, I pray
for strength buoyed by the presence of this gift received.
Late October's golden leaves holding fast to limbs in sprays.
Kept from falling by the warmth of extra days.

Haiku

My conversations
tell past capers   I long for
new stories to share

Passages

Tanglewood calls me   has called me for years
a timpani reverberating from the hills
a solo flute in call and response with territorial birds
the Boston Symphony freed from its hall
violins in rhythm with the wind

A two-hour flight from my house   a day-and-a-half's drive
still I've not been there   not yet

Came close once half a lifetime ago I in a prairie skirt
he in a tie dye tee buckled into our low-slung sports car
pulling a tiny blue camper   I worried we wouldn't fit among
the crisp white shirts creased trousers so we pushed on past
Tanglewood to a low-budget campground

Came close a dozen years later a sedan this time
an eight-year-old buckled into the back seat
his mitt and ball in hand a bat beside him
again it didn't seem time   on our way
to the Baseball Hall of Fame

I listened for the timpani the solo flute
thought I heard a viola in the wind

Half a lifetime and more I signed up for a tour
alone this time at ease in a crisp white shirt flowing crop pants
but the pandemic hit   the tour canceled   I stayed home
imagined settling into outdoor seating
shadows from the waning light at play

Nearing a lifetime now I wonder should I try once more slip with
my walker into the back row   listen for that viola in the wind

many paths lead
from free space lull us with choice
all require coin

About the Author

Kathleen Serley is a lifelong Wisconsin resident and retired educator. She has a Ph.D. from UW-Madison and serves as Mid-Central VP for Wisconsin Fellowship of Poets. Her poems appear in journals including *The Solitary Plover, Third Wednesday, Verse Wisconsin,* and *Eastern Iowa Review* and have been recognized by The Hal Prize, Verse and Visions, and the UWEC Centennial Poetry Competition. Her first book of poetry, *Statements Made in Passing,* was released in Spring 2022.

www.ingramcontent.com/pod-product-compliance
Lightning Source LLC
Chambersburg PA
CBHW031008090426
42737CB00008B/730